Barbara Brackman and Karla Menaugh

Emporia Rose
APPLIQUÉ QUILTS

New Projects, Historical Vignettes, Classic Designs

Text copyright © 2014 by Barbara Brackman and Karla Menaugh

Photography and Artwork copyright © 2014 by C&T Publishing, Inc.

Publisher: Amy Marson

Creative Director: Gailen Runge

Art Director: Kristy Zacharias

Editors: S. Michele Fry and Monica Gyulai

Technical Editors: Ellen Pahl and Amanda Siegfried

Cover/Book Designer: April Mostek

Page Layout Artist: Katie McIntosh

Production Coordinator: Rue Flaherty

Production Editor: Alice Mace Nakanishi

Illustrator: Mary E. Flynn

Photo Assistant: Mary Peyton Peppo

Instructional photography by Diane Pedersen, unless otherwise noted

Published by C&T Publishing, Inc., P.O. Box 1456, Lafayette, CA 94549

Library of Congress Cataloging-in-Publication Data

Brackman, Barbara.

 Emporia Rose appliqué quilts : new projects, historical vignettes, classic designs / Barbara Brackman and Karla Menaugh.

    pages cm

 ISBN 978-1-60705-890-8 (soft cover)

1. Quilting--Patterns. 2. Appliqué--Patterns. I. Menaugh, Karla, 1954- II. Title.

 TT835.B639 2014

 746.46--dc23

                            2013040404

Printed in China

10 9 8 7 6 5 4 3 2 1

Acknowledgments

We want to thank everyone who has made an *Emporia Rose Sampler*, including class members at the Common Threads Quilt Shop in Waxahachie, Texas, and at Prairie Point Quilts in Shawnee, Kansas. We show a few of them here, but many more were made.

We also want to thank the staff at the Denver Art Museum and the Spencer Museum of Art at the University of Kansas. Both museums have been very generous over the years in sharing their quilt treasures. The archives at the Lyon County Historical Museum (Emporia, Kansas) have been helpful too—painting a picture of Emporia almost 100 years ago.

In the 1980s, Mary Kretsinger, daughter of key Emporia quilter Rose Kretsinger, spent a good deal of time discussing her mother and her work, as did Mrs. Harold Becker, niece of Charlotte Whitehill—another of Emporia's prominent quiltmakers. We also are grateful to the Kansas Quilt Project, which sponsored numerous interviews with family members of other Emporia quiltmakers, helping us gain insight into an impressive quilting community.

Contents

Commercial Street, Emporia, Kansas, about 1905

The *Emporia Rose Sampler* celebrates the women in a Kansas community who created a unique group of quilts in the 1920s, '30s, and '40s. Their quilts have been published around the world as ideal examples of design and workmanship. Three women have been recognized for their roles in this artistic movement: Rose Good Kretsinger, whose work is now in the Spencer Museum of Art at the University of Kansas; Charlotte Jane Whitehill, whose quilts are at the Denver Art Museum; and Josephine Craig, who has three quilts at the Kansas Museum of History. The works of several other equally talented appliqué artists remain in their families.

We first became aware of the Emporia quiltmaking community in 1985 when the Kansas Quilt Project traveled around the state documenting quilts. We discovered that many of the most dynamic mid-twentieth-century quilts had some link to that one town. Those Emporia quilts were a product of their place and time.

The Place

Opening the streetcar line in 1911

Emporia, in the grass-covered Flint Hills of eastern Kansas, was founded in 1857 by easterners with free-state sympathies before the Civil War. The name comes from the Greek word for "marketplace," a concept the town exemplified in the late nineteenth and early twentieth centuries when it thrived on railroads and cattle.

But Emporia was much more than a cow town. Settled by relatively wealthy New Englanders, it boasted two institutions of higher education and an opera house. Nicknamed the "Athens of Kansas" by William Allen White, the *Emporia Gazette*'s prominent Pulitzer Prize–winning editor, it became known as a place with a well-educated, sophisticated population that held on to front-porch, main-street values.

White, who hobnobbed with movers and shakers in politics, business, and the arts, played a role in boosting the reputation of Emporia's outstanding quilters. His paper regularly reported on their victories at quilt shows.

Postcard, showing popular poet Walt Mason on his front porch, about 1910. The homey rhymes that "Uncle Walt" wrote for the *Gazette* were well liked nationally. With his royalties, he soon built a much larger house.

A ribbon in a crazy quilt recalls a 1902 convention of traveling salesmen in Emporia. Newman's Department Store supplied the souvenirs to members of the United Commercial Travelers, a fraternal and lobbying group. Rose Kretsinger's father was a traveling salesman around this time.

William Allen White in front of *Gazette* offices, 1924

In our Kansas Quilt Project interviews we learned about farm wives who quilted together in the country around Emporia and about individuals, such as Josephine Craig, who retired from farm to town and began to make quilts for shows. We also heard about the quilters who finished the elegant appliquéd tops. Most were sewing for others because they needed the money; they charged by the yard of thread used in the stitching.

Clearly, quilting in Emporia drew together women from many walks of life, but class differences still kept them apart. While most were acquainted with one another through clubs or churches, they were not a close-knit community of friends. Some shared patterns and many shared the same quilters—the unsung women who finished the quilts. Quite a few shared a spirit of competition, keeping their latest work secret until the fall agricultural fairs.

Photo by Russell Lee, courtesy of the Library of Congress

Gonzales County Fair, Texas, 1939

White liked to celebrate Emporia as egalitarian, but class differences are evident in his paper and in the quilters' social circles. He characterized the *Gazette*'s audience as "the best people of the city." These prominent citizens included quiltmakers, such as Rose Kretsinger, Jennie Soden, and Ifie Arnold, whose husbands worked in law, banking, and business. Even during the Great Depression they had money for the best supplies from Kansas City and Topeka, and they had time to appliqué intricate designs. When they couldn't find suitable fabric, they ordered better cotton from London.

These women set the trends, but many women of "lower classes" also made spectacular quilts. Among these quilters were Charlotte Jane Whitehill, an insurance agent, and Ruth Lee, a seamstress who helped support her family by remaking worn men's suits into women's clothing.

Emporia's quilters "vied against each other," according to one daughter, with the textile division at the Lyon County Fair a prime spot for competition. Everyone entered the Lyon County Fair. Many won prizes at the state fairs; and a few, including Josephine Craig and Rose Kretsinger, won national contests. One reason

Emporia was such a quilting hotbed was that the *Gazette*, in its mission to boost the town, kindled the spirit of competition under the recurring headline "Emporia Gets In."

The Period

The time span for these impressive quilts, 1925–1945, also contributed to the Emporia phenomenon. While those years were not particularly good times for Kansas farmers nor the towns that depended on their trade, they did coincide with a boom period for innovations in design and needlework. Quilt historians mark the late 1920s as the beginning of an American quilt revival, in which women were caught up in a patchwork fad. Rose Kretsinger and her mother, Anna Good, took up the craft just as needlework editors began to respond to the growing interest in an old craft.

Americans were infatuated with Colonial nostalgia. Homemakers embraced quilts, rag rugs, and embroidered samplers because they went beyond mere interior decoration; they exemplified America's glorious past. While these new quilters sometimes drew upon designs from the 1850s even as they touted "Colonial" spirit, the movement wasn't so much rooted in a particular historical period (nor historical accuracy!) as it was about participating with one's needle in a crafts revival.

Revival implies new life, so the quilt craze demanded a new look, a modern look. The needlework magazine *Modern Priscilla* captured the paradox of current ideas mixed with tradition, not only in its name but also in its editorial policies that promised projects "quaintly gay in a modern way."

Innovative ideas from art nouveau to Bauhaus design were changing both manufactured and handmade objects. Rose Kretsinger, with a college education in arts and crafts design and a year spent in Europe before World War I, was particularly poised to add modern design ideas to traditional patchwork. Like many other seamstresses, she responded to the popular demand for traditional yet modern quilts by combining parts of both ideas. But her synthesis was distinctive—old patterns with new colors, antique calicoes in thoughtful compositions, and old needlework standards with art nouveau borders.

Emporia Gets In

Two quilts of old Colonial pattern, made by Mrs. M. R. Craig, took first prizes at the Topeka fair and first and sweepstake prizes at the Hutchinson [state] fair this fall. Two quilts of original design made by Mrs. Roy Lee, which won first and second prizes at the Topeka fair, in the original design division, also took first honors in that division at the Hutchinson fair.

—*Emporia Gazette,* September 24, 1934

Rose Good Kretsinger

Rose Good Kretsinger (1886–1963), with daughter, Mary, about 1916

Rose attended the Art Institute of Chicago and graduated in 1908. After a year in Europe, she designed jewelry and fabric in Chicago. In 1914 she moved to Emporia and married widower William S. Kretsinger, an attorney and rancher. Rose and Will had two children, Mary Amelia, born in 1915, and William DeVere, born in 1917.

Katy Station, about the time Rose arrived in Emporia

We named our appliqué sampler *Emporia Rose* after the woman who was the heart of the quilting community. Rose Frances Good was born to Milton and Anna Gleissner Good, in Hope, Kansas, near the cattle town of Abilene. The family moved to Abilene, Kansas, and then to Kansas City, Missouri.

Rose's father was a merchant, whose fortunes rose and fell with booms in cattle and land. He'd been a partner with David Eisenhower, but after their store failed they went separate ways. Eisenhower moved to Texas, where his son, the future president of the United States, was born.

Rose brought her unique background as a professionally trained artist to quiltmaking. She quickly won local and national fame with a combination of old-fashioned standards and modern design. The Kansas City Art Institute exhibited her quilts in the early 1930s, and in 1935 she published *The Romance of the Patchwork Quilt in America* with Carrie Hall.

After Rose's death, her daughter donated twelve of her quilts to the Spencer Museum of Art in Lawrence, Kansas, where they continue to delight quilt lovers. Rose was innovative, competitive, and willing to share her ideas through hand-drawn patterns and one-on-one assistance. With her talent, training, and generosity, she was central to the Emporia quilting phenomenon.

Charlotte Jane Whitehill

Charlotte (Lottie) as a young woman, about 1890

Charlotte Jane Cline Whitehill grew up in Wisconsin surrounded by quilts. Her mother, Elizabeth Ann Cline (1842–1935), was a quilter too. Lottie, as family and friends called her, didn't begin making quilts in earnest until she was in her 60s. Inspired by Rose Kretsinger, Lottie made a parallel quilt to each of Kretsinger's and also adapted several antique patterns on her own.

When Lottie donated her quilts to the Denver Art Museum, she also donated several quilts made by her mother. She recalled that patterns were sometimes difficult to obtain and was quoted in the 1964 museum catalog as saying, "Strategy was often required to obtain permission to copy them." In one case, she reported, "I just talked it away from them."

Lottie spent much of her adult life in Kansas as a professional woman, married to George Whitehill. She was elected clerk of Coffey County and served as an agent and a district manager for an insurance company.

She began to quilt after George's death. While visiting clients in small towns around Emporia, she took the opportunity to shop at local dry goods stores, where she kept her eye out for old-fashioned fabrics, such as the indigo blue print she used in *Spice Pink* (page 14).

Charlotte Jane Whitehill (1866–1964) about 1950, with her version of the quilt *Paradise Garden*, current location unknown

About 1940 Lottie moved to Denver to live near her niece. In 1955, when the time came to donate her quilts, she chose the city's museum of art. The Cline-Whitehill quilts became the focus of an important quilt collection. The museum has 19 of Lottie's quilts. She mentioned 22 in a Christmas poem in 1941, and in 1955 she told museum staff she'd completed 36 tops.

"Like the warmth of my quilts on a cold, winter night
Like their lovely designs so colorful and bright
Like each painstaking stitch in all twenty-two
Are my very best Holiday wishes for you."

—Christmas card from Lottie Whitehill, 1941

Anna Gleissner Good

Abilene in 1875, the year the Gleissners arrived

Anna Gleissner was born in 1865, the year her parents moved to the United States from Bavaria. Though she was a quilter herself, Anna's significance to the Emporia quilt phenomenon is largely due to her influence on her daughter, Rose Kretsinger.

When Anna was ten years old, her parents settled in Abilene, Kansas, and Anna grew up with six brothers and sisters in a classic American cow town. She taught school in her late teens and at twenty married Milton D. Good, who co-owned a dry goods store in nearby Hope, Kansas, with David Eisenhower.

Thomas Branigar, who studied the Good-Eisenhower partnership, found references to Milton as handsome, enterprising, and congenial; nevertheless, he said that Good did not get along with Eisenhower. After a few years their contentious partnership broke up, with lasting bad feelings. Eisenhower family stories depicted Milton Good as deceitful, but Branigar found no evidence of villainy on either side. The relationship might have been

forgotten except for the fact that David Eisenhower's son, Dwight, became a famous soldier and later president of the United States. Family animosity toward Milton Good was set in print in General Eisenhower's 1945 biography, which must have caused Milton's daughter, Rose, some heartache.

Milton may have been enterprising, but he had a hard time making a living. After the partnership failed and the Goods' only child, Rose Frances, was born in Hope in 1886, the family returned to Abilene, where Milton opened another store. During the economic troubles of the 1890s, the family moved in with Anna's parents. Lawsuits and bankruptcy colored Rose's childhood, but by the time she was ready for an extended education, the Goods could afford to send her to the Art Institute of Chicago and afterward for a year of European study, where her mother, Anna, joined her for a bicycling tour.

After Rose married in 1914, Anna and her husband, whose health was failing, moved to Emporia to live with their daughter. Milton died a few years later. Anna spent some time in the early 1920s in Eskridge, Kansas, keeping house for one of her brothers and making quilts. She later returned to Emporia, where she worked as a sorority housemother and maintained a close relationship with Rose. They shared a love of needlework, and Rose consulted her mother when working on quilts. Walking home from Rose's house in October 1926, Anna was killed by a drunken driver, and Rose was devastated.

Inspiration from Emporia

Above, clockwise from top left: Details of *Pennsylvania Garden* (page 38), *Anna's Thistle* (page 40), *Perennial Poppy* (page 34), and *Spice Pink Table Runner* (page 46)

Emporia Rose Sampler, 87˝ × 87˝, made by Denise Lipscomb, quilted by Sabina Thompson, 2011

The quilts in this book celebrate the unique work of a group of Kansas quiltmakers from the 1920s, '30s, and '40s, whose quilts have been published around the world as ideal examples of design and workmanship. The quilts in this chapter inspired Barbara Brackman to design the *Emporia Rose Sampler* and several related quilts and needlework projects. You can use her designs to re-create your own version of one of the projects, or follow the tips in Bonus Ideas (pages 52–55) to make your own design inspired by these truly incredible quilts.

New Rose Tree

88¾″ × 86½″, made by Rose Good Kretsinger, hand quilter unknown, 1929

New Rose Tree is the inspiration for

· **New Rose Wreath block** (next page) in *Emporia Rose Sampler* (page 30)

New Rose Wreath Block

New Rose Wreath block from *Emporia Rose Sampler* (page 30)

The New Rose Wreath block is adapted from the center of Kretsinger's *New Rose Tree*, which won a first prize at the 1930 Kansas State Fair. The quilt was published in the Hall and Kretsinger book, *The Romance of the Patchwork Quilt in America*, where it's called *Rose Tree* and captioned, "This is a modern version of a very old pattern with original center and border swag." The wreath from the center of that quilt is repeated four times as the alternate block in our *Emporia Rose Sampler*.

Rose saw the flowers in this traditional appliqué design as rose buds, but we might view them as "love apples" or pomegranates. The patterns in the blocks and borders date back to the 1840s, and Rose's use of antique and reproduction fabrics gives a sense of the traditional red and green appliqué that was her inspiration.

Rose kept a list of her quilts and their prizes in her copy of Marie Webster's 1915 book *Quilts: Their Story and How to Make Them*. The quilt is called *New Rose Tree* and dated 1929 here. Quilt historian Joyce Gross photographed the book for her magazine *Quilters' Journal*, number 31.

Spice Pink

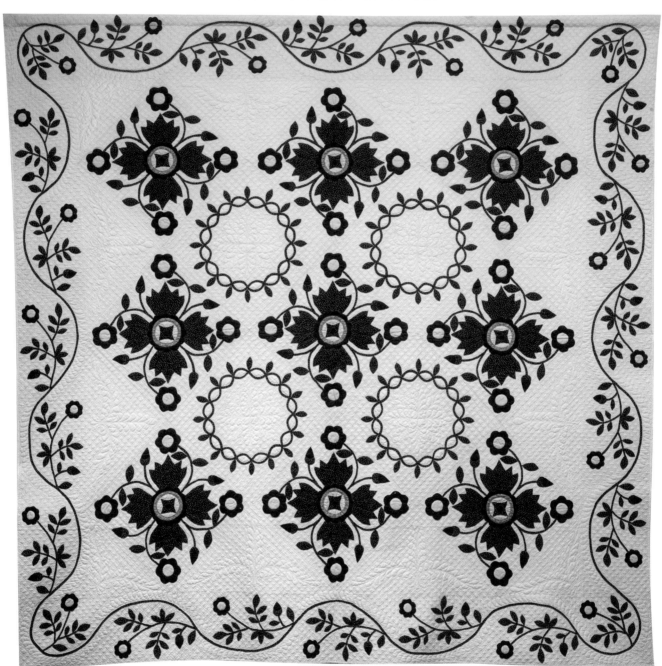

84″ × 86″, made by Charlotte Jane Whitehill, hand quilter unknown, 1932

Spice Pink is the inspiration for

- Spice Pink block (next page) in *Emporia Rose Sampler* (page 30)

- *Spice Pink Table Runner* (page 46)

- *Spice Pink Variation* quilt (page 53) and *Emporia Rose with Spice Pink Border* (page 54) in Bonus Ideas (page 52)

Spice Pink Block

Spice Pink block from *Emporia Rose Sampler* (page 30)

Carnation.
Dianthus caryophyllus plenus.

Spice pink is an old-fashioned name for a dianthus or carnation.

Spice Pink has much in common with Rose Kretsinger's *Calendula* (page 26), made the same year. Each alternates a floral block with a simpler wreath, a graceful setting adopted for our *Emporia Rose Sampler* (page 30). Lottie often set her blocks on point, a design technique quite common in nineteenth-century quilts; Rose did not often use it. Blocks on point make the Whitehill quilt look more old-fashioned than the Kretsinger quilts.

For the Spice Pink border, Lottie used a traditional vine that adds to the nineteenth-century illusion. We have included a pattern for the Spice Pink border (pullout page P1) as an alternative to our more modern Pride of Emporia border used in *Emporia Rose Sampler*. This floral block is a variation of the traditional *Democrat Rose* design, a stylized blossom with whirling arms and four cockscombs radiating from the center. Quilt historian Florence Peto, writing in the 1940s, speculated that the comb shape represented the Democrats' rooster. We're familiar with the Democratic donkey, but the rooster was the party's mid-nineteenth-century symbol.

Spice Pink, the Emporia name for this rose variation, is curious. Lottie's quilt is red, yellow, and indigo blue with just a touch of double pink print in the ring in the center. Did she imagine the cockscombs looked like carnations, or *pinks*? Pinks didn't have to be pink; the name refers to the serrated or pinked edge to the blossoms.

A note on the back of the Whitehill quilt says the quilting contains 1,419 yards of thread. Lottie probably knew that because professional quilters often charged by the yard of thread used.

Indian Paintbrush

89˝ × 88˝, made by Charlotte Jane Whitehill, hand quilter unknown, 1934

Indian Paintbrush is the inspiration for

- Indian Paintbrush block (next page) in *Emporia Rose Sampler* (page 30)

Indian Paintbrush Block

Indian Paintbrush block from *Emporia Rose Sampler* (page 30)

Indian Paintbrush

Charlotte Whitehill's inspiration was an antique appliqué belonging to Stephen and Hulda Rich, who lived across the street from Rose Kretsinger.

This appliqué block is a variation of a mid-nineteenth-century favorite commonly named *Rose Wreath* or *President's Wreath*. But it was called *Indian Paintbrush* in Emporia, named after a bright orange wildflower native to the Kansas prairies. The original quilt belonging to the Riches was made in 1852 when Kansas was still Indian territory. It is highly unlikely, however, that the quilt is a Kansas native because so few European American women lived in the territory then. Like most other nineteenth-century appliqué quilts in Emporia, the quilt was probably brought from the East.

Hulda (1862–1949) and her husband, Stephen (1849–1942), were cousins from Indiana. The quilt had belonged to Stephen's mother, Hannah Hinshaw Rich. Their granddaughter recalled that Rose Kretsinger and her neighbors worked together with Stephen doing the quilting on Hulda's quilts. The *Emporia Gazette* described Stephen Rich as "an accomplished quilter" when the couple displayed nine of their quilts at the Emporia Fall Frolic in the 1930s, including "two quilts which Mr. Rich quilted when he was twenty years old and was sick all winter with whooping cough."

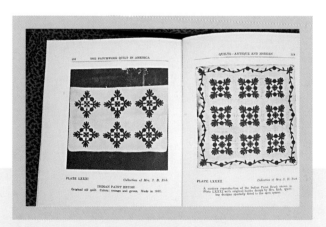

Photos from the 1935 Hall and Kretsinger book show the antique quilt on the left with Hulda Rich's 1930s interpretation on the right. Here we can see how Emporia's appliqué artists exchanged ideas and altered sets and borders. Rich and Whitehill each rearranged the block's floral components to make a distinctive border.

Rose mentioned him circuitously in *Romance*: "Even the men stop to reminisce when they see a quilt displayed. One man whom I happen to know has been interested enough in his wife's quiltmaking to assist in the quilting of a pattern which belonged to his mother, the work being rendered the more interesting by the use of her original quilting frame which had lain away in the attic of their ancestral home these many years."

The Riches' version of *Indian Paintbrush* was published in the February 1949 issue of *Farm Journal*, which offered patterns for three Emporia quilts for a quarter each.

Tomato Flower

Denver Art Museum Neusteter Textile Collection, Gift of Charlotte Jane Whitehill, 1955.66

84″ × 86″, made by Charlotte Jane Whitehill, hand quilter unknown, 1931

Tomato Flower is the inspiration for

- Tomato Flower block (next page) in *Emporia Rose Sampler* (page 30)

- Leaf border in *Emporia Rose Sampler*

- Tomato Buds Pincushion (page 50)

- *Heirloom Tomato Flower* (page 53) in Bonus Ideas (page 52)

Tomato Flower Block

Tomato Flower block from *Emporia Rose Sampler* (page 30)

This pattern was copied from an antique quilt that belonged to the Martindales, an Emporia banking family with roots in Ohio and Illinois. At least two versions were made in Emporia, one by Charlotte Whitehill and one by Jennie Soden. Jennie's daughter, Margaret ("Peg" to her family), recalled that the Soden version was used and worn out. Lottie's *Tomato Flower* is in the Denver Art Museum today.

Cherry tomato

We haven't found a picture of the inspiration quilt. The block looks familiar, with its central flower in the classic eight-lobed shape and four arms extending into corners that sprout tulips—or are those lilies? The pale yellow tomato flowers in our gardens aren't nearly as spectacular as this, but the name may come from the bright fruit in the blocks and border—cherry tomatoes?

In our block design, we simplified Lottie's block by shortening the stems a bit. We guess her original quilt used blocks about 24˝. Placed on point with an 8˝ finished border, five blocks would have made a quilt sized for a double bed. Her border is similar to our Pride of Emporia border (pullout page P3). Having the leaves crossing over a straight line seems inspired by Rose Kretsinger's signature style. The geometry of the straight lines and the circular dots adds a rather modern look to the traditional pattern.

Soden's Mill and Grove in the 1880s

The Sodens were among Emporia's founding families. Emporia lost a landmark when the Soden mill on the banks of the Cottonwood River burned down in the 1930s. Jennie Perley Soden (1872–1959) made several quilts together with her daughter using patterns from her friends. Margaret remembered that her mother kept a strict eye on her appliqué stitches and was proud that their work looked identical.

Spencer Museum of Art, The University of Kansas, Gift of Mary Kretsinger, 1971.0093

85˝ × 86½˝, made by Rose Good Kretsinger, hand quilter unknown, 1927

Oriental Poppy is the inspiration for

- **Oriental Poppy block (next page) in *Emporia Rose Sampler* (page 30)**
- *Perennial Poppy* **(page 34)**
- **Oriental Poppy Pincushion (page 50)**
- *Antique Oriental Poppy* **(page 54) in Bonus Ideas (page 52)**

Oriental Poppy Block

Oriental Poppy block from *Emporia Rose Sampler* (page 30)

"Although [the] modern type of quilting has no serious merit, it still finds its way into every home in village, town, and city, because of the little difficulty encountered in the making. What a pity, for it would be really more worthwhile to spend years in the making of one good piece of quilting than the time it takes to quilt all the other inartistic ones."

—Rose Kretsinger, *The Romance of the Patchwork Quilt in America*, 1935

The *Oriental Poppy* looks to be Rose's third quilt, the first that she drew based on an antique quilt in an Emporia collection. In her list of prizes she noted that it won first prize at Topeka's statewide fair in 1931.

Always eager to boost Emporians, the *Gazette* in 1930 featured a story about Rose Kretsinger and her prize-winning quilts, describing this quilt as "a copy of an old pattern, which is nameless, but which Mrs. Kretsinger calls the Oriental Poppy because it is composed of poppy-like red flowers and heavy leaves. The pattern for the quilt was provided by a maid in the Kretsinger home, and has a long and romantic history.... About 75 years ago a grandmother of the girl stored her hope chest in her Chicago home just before her wedding. The home burned in the great Chicago fire, and only fragments of the furnishings remained in the ashes. The hope chest was destroyed, but smoldering pieces of the folded quilts it contained were preserved. The girl inherited these tattered pieces as souvenirs, and Mrs. Kretsinger was able to sketch two patterns from them."

The pattern seems to have been taken from a fairly popular mid-nineteenth-century design found in quilts from Maryland to Ohio. Pairs of serrated leaves often grow out of a central fleur-de-lis shape. Rose saw it as a poppy although one could argue that it's a rose. She used reverse appliqué to indicate the layers in the flowers, but you can add those in regular appliqué if you like.

The maid's charred quilt must have been a sampler of different patterns, with at least two of the designs having survived. In a 1949 *Farm Journal* article offering Rose's pattern, Reba Marshall wrote: "She gets most of the ideas for her designs by looking at old quilts.... Each block [having] a different design, Mrs. Kretsinger takes just one of these blocks and designs an entire quilt from it.... [It] makes a neater looking spread with a single theme."

A few years ago we bought a box of patterns from a woman in Emporia. In it we found hand-drawn designs in an envelope labeled "Mrs. Kretsinger's Pattern" and also "Mrs. Kretsinger's Gift." We've drawn the *Oriental Poppy* pattern here from that tissue-paper pattern, leaving the slashes in the poppy leaves. Although Rose didn't slash the leaves in her quilt, it's a good place for more reverse appliqué.

Pennsylvania Beauty

70¹/₁₆″ × 70⅞″, unfinished quilt top, made by Rose Good Kretsinger, 1931

Pennsylvania Beauty is the inspiration for

- Pennsylvania Beauty block (next page) in *Emporia Rose Sampler* (page 30)
- *Pennsylvania Garden* (page 38)

Pennsylvania Beauty Block

Pennsylvania Beauty block from *Emporia Rose Sampler* (page 30)

"It has been said by different disinterested people: 'Why spend so much time and labor making new quilts and worrying about designs when you already have a number which are never used?' Perhaps it is for the same reason which prompts the planting of flowers in the alley, back of the garden fence."

—Rose Kretsinger, *The Romance of the Patchwork Quilt in America*, 1935

Rose Kretsinger, about 1950

In the mid-1970s, Rose Kretsinger's daughter, Mary, took this unfinished top to the Spencer Museum of Art. It is most likely the *Pennsylvania Beauty* or *Pennsylvania Garden* listed in Rose's accounts as "My design—old calico, flowers & berries in lavender." It's numbered both 16 and 17 on her list. Perhaps she started another that was also never finished.

Rose placed the block on point in the center of a full-sized top and began to fill in the corners with appliqué. For our interpretation of her quilt idea, see *Pennsylvania Garden* (page 38). We simplified the center block here for our last sampler pattern.

The inspiration for the block may have been an antique quilt from Pennsylvania, where the women of German ancestry are famed for their appliqué designs, which are usually based on traditional Germanic folk arts. Design principles include color schemes relying on the complements of red and green, flat symbolic florals based on eight-pointed stars or eight-lobed rosettes, and mirror-image symmetries in which the corners of the designs reflect each other. Design elements often rotate around a central image in a whirling cross format that packs a good deal of detail into a square.

Rose did not keep up her intensive quilt production after she and Carrie Hall published *The Romance of the Patchwork Quilt* in 1935, perhaps because of family obligations. Her children were teenagers in the early 1930s. Biographer Jonathan Gregory mentions animosity between Rose and Carrie Hall over royalties from the book, suggesting that may have diminished her joy in quiltmaking. However, Mary told us in an interview that Rose had a hand tremor and it affected her sewing skills so that they were no longer up to her exacting standards. A few years after her husband's death in 1940, Rose finished one more top, *Paradise Garden*. Whatever her reasons, the *Pennsylvania Beauty* top was never completed and a threaded needle remains in place where she left it.

Indiana Wreath and Pride of Iowa

Indiana Wreath from Marie D. Webster's 1915 book, *Quilts: Their Story and How to Make Them*. Inspired by this colorplate of the original quilt made in 1858, several Emporia quiltmakers made their own versions of the *Indiana Wreath* quilt.

Rose Kretsinger's *Pride of Iowa* was shown on her inherited four-poster bed in *The Romance of the Patchwork Quilt*. She always said she was inspired to make quilts because she wanted a period bedcover for this antique bed brought from Pennsylvania by her father.

Indiana Wreath and **Pride of Iowa** are the inspiration for

- Pride of Emporia border (next page) in *Emporia Rose Sampler* (page 30)

Pride of Emporia Border

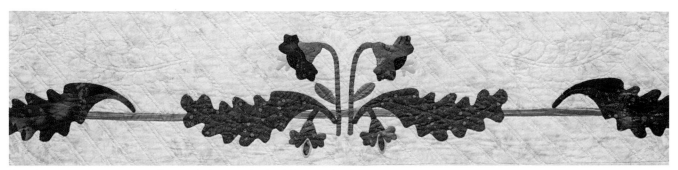

Detail of *Emporia Rose Sampler* (page 30) showing Pride of Emporia border

Detail of *Emporia Rose Sampler* made by Ina Mae Carney (page 26)

Emporia borders included graceful corners, as these quilts were designed to be seen both on a wall in contests and on a bed.

In fact, you can spot an Emporia quilt by its borders. They feature distinctive, often sophisticated designs that owe as much to art nouveau as to traditional quilt design. The hand of Rose Kretsinger, who was a professional jewelry designer, is evident in the graceful leaves of this pattern, which is taken from the border on her *Pride of Iowa*. Charlotte Jane Whitehill used a similar leaf laid over a straight line for her *Tomato Flower* (page 18). For our sampler, we added a bouquet at the bottom, inspired by the flowers in the border of *Indiana Wreath*.

"In reviewing some of the old specimens of quilting displayed in our museums and private collections, we stand amazed at the manifestations of harmonious form and order."

—Rose Kretsinger, *The Romance of the Patchwork Quilt in America*, 1935

Calendula

88½″ × 89¾″, made by Rose Good Kretsinger, hand quilter unknown, 1930–1932

Spencer Museum of Art, The University of Kansas, Gift of Mary Kretsinger, 1971.0096

Emporia Rose Sampler, 87″ × 87″, made by Ina Mae Carney, hand quilted by Anne Thomas, 2004

Our *Emporia Rose Sampler*, set with alternate wreaths, was inspired by the *Calendula* quilt. Rose Kretsinger set four geometric wreaths among five florals, which she called *Calendula*. A calendula is a kind of marigold, the inspiration for the coloring in her bright orange flowers.

Rose initially called it *Democratic Rose and Rings* in a note written on the paper pattern now at the Spencer Museum of Art. A *Democratic Rose* might have been appropriate for the Allens, the family whose quilt inspired Rose to make her version. Harry K. Allen, a law school dean when Rose borrowed the quilt, went on to become the state's first Democratic Supreme Court Justice. Rose's husband, however, was a Republican politician, so we can imagine that a name change might have been well advised. The quilt was later called *Calendula* or *Allen Rose*.

Calendula is the inspiration for

- **Nine-block setting with alternate wreaths in *Emporia Rose Sampler* (page 30)**
- **Social Circles Pillow (page 48)**

Double Irish Chain and Scotch Thistle

Spencer Museum of Art, The University of Kansas, Gift of Mary Kretsinger, 1971.0105

69¼˝ × 81½˝, made by Anna Gleissner Good, 1925

Double Irish Chain and Scotch Thistle is the inspiration for

- *Anna's Thistle* (page 40)
- **Thistle and Buds Pincushions** (page 50)

Anna Gleissner Good made her *Double Irish Chain and Scotch Thistle* quilt in 1925 for her grandson, Bill. Her inspiration was a thistle pattern, advertised as "bound to appeal to masculine taste" in *The Priscilla Patchwork Book*.

Hand Quilting Traditions

Many Emporia women hired professional hand quilters to finish their quilts, a traditional division of labor. Some appliqué artists marked their tops with their trademark quilting designs before sending them to the quilter because they feared handing over templates that might be copied. But, of course, a good quilter could easily trace the patterns from the top, so many of the best designs were the stock in trade of these talented artisans.

Quilters' names were well guarded because a good needlewoman who could take direction would soon be overscheduled if everyone knew about her. Because of this secrecy, and the fact that the best designs were passed around, it's hard to identify just who quilted what. As a result, the quilters have received little credit. Their anonymity is an injustice because their stitches are as important as the appliqué work in making Emporia quilts the masterpieces they are.

The best work was thought to be that of a skilled individual rather than a quilting group like a church organization, in which stitch size might vary. The Fowler sisters, Eugenia and Grace, are often mentioned as professional quilters who might have finished the Kretsinger and Whitehill pieces. "Grandma" Fannie Moon is another candidate. In 1937, the *Emporia Gazette* printed a story about her, noting "she has quilted many quilts for other women, too, and could be busy all the time at this work, but she likes to take her time, refuses to be hurried.… She enjoys making the tiny stitches and watching the feather and scroll, hearts and rounds and compass, and other designs grow under her skilled fingers."

Needlecraft of Two Emporians Wins Prizes

Mrs. M. R. Craig and Mrs. W. S. Kretsinger were named Wednesday, in New York City, among the prize-winning exhibitors of handicrafts and needlework at the annual Women's International Exposition of Arts and Industries, currently at Madison Square Garden.

—Emporia Gazette, November 30, 1942

Quilting around a frame in Scranton, Iowa, about 1940

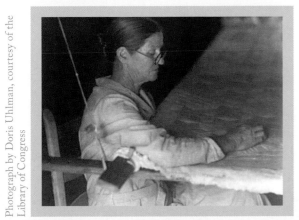

Unknown woman quilting, about 1930

Rose Kretsinger's quilting suggestions from *Romance*

Emporia quilts inspired the quilting patterns included throughout this book. Rose Kretsinger was undoubtedly the source for the design ideas, which she drew from antique quilts. She outlined her ideas in her section of *The Romance of the Patchwork Quilt in America*. Rose had a wonderful way with feathers, which she broke up into units rather than continuing a single feather around the border, to make spacing and marking easier. She also focused on corners, designing motifs from which the feathers grew.

Made and hand quilted by Cindy Korb, 2003

Emporia Rose Sampler

Finished quilt: 87″ × 87″ | **Finished block:** 21″

The *Emporia Rose Sampler* was designed by Barbara Brackman based on several Emporia quilts. The sampler she created alternates five floral blocks with four identical wreaths, all drawn from designs shared among quiltmakers in the town of Emporia, Kansas, in the decades between the World Wars. It's framed by the Pride of Emporia border, an Emporia-inspired appliquéd border that is a trademark of these quilts.

Fabric Requirements and Cutting Instructions

Because the appliqué process tends to shrink blocks and borders slightly, the block backgrounds are cut oversized. You will trim them to size after the appliqué is finished. For more information about preparing and cutting the background fabric, see Fabric Preparation (page 56). Yardage is based on 42″-wide fabric.

Before tracing and cutting appliqué shapes, see Appliqué (page 56). Refer to the patterns (pullout pages P1–P4) and to the color photo of the quilt (previous page) as a guide to color placement.

EMPORIA ROSE SAMPLER

Fabric	For	Cutting
¾ yard each of 9 yellows*	Block backgrounds	1 square 23″ × 23″ from each
5¼ yards mottled yellow	Border	4 strips 12½″ × 93″
	Binding	4 strips 2½″ × 93″
½ yard brown	Accent border strip	10 strips 1½″ × width of fabric
⅜ yard assorted oranges	Flowers, buds, and berries	See *Emporia Rose Sampler* block and border patterns (pullout pages P1–P4).
¼ yard assorted yellows		
¾ yard assorted reds	Flowers, buds, berries, and border leaves	
1¼ yards assorted purples		
2 yards assorted greens	Leaves, stems, vines, wreaths, and flower parts	
⅜ yard assorted browns	Leaves, stems, and flower parts	
8 yards neutral	Backing	
96″ × 96″ batting		

* Cindy cut the center background square from the same fabric she used in the border. Purchase an extra ¾ yard of border fabric if you want to do the same.

Blocks

1. Appliqué 4 New Rose Wreath blocks and 1 block each of Indian Paintbrush, Spice Pink, Pennsylvania Beauty, Tomato Flower, and Oriental Poppy. Use your favorite appliqué technique to stitch the blocks. For more information about our techniques, see Appliqué (page 56).

2. Trim each block to 21½″ × 21½″, making sure the design is centered.

3. Arrange the blocks in 3 rows of 3 blocks each, and sew them together.

"Sometimes my friends wonder how I get so many [quilts] done. But making quilts is the only thing I have ever found that I could do while listening to the radio or visiting. I have my materials all ready, fixing them in moments when I am not busy, and then each day I work on them in odd moments when I am cooking, or waiting for callers, or catching a few minutes' rest."

— Rose Kretsinger, *Emporia Gazette*, September 16, 1930

Borders

1. Piece the 1½″ brown accent strips together end to end to make a single long strip. Cut the strip into 4 strips 1½″ × 93″.

2. Fold each accent strip in half, right sides together, to make a ¾″-wide strip, and press.

3. With a removable marker and ruler, mark a line on a 12½″ border strip that is 4¼″ from what will be the outer edge of the quilt. Place an accent strip on the border, having raw edges even with the marked line and facing the inner edge of the border. Pin in place and stitch ¼″ away from the raw edges.

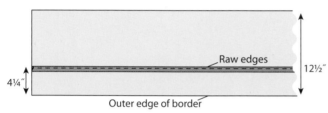

Add accent border.

4. Flip the strip over the stitching so that no raw edges are showing. Appliqué the other edge. Repeat for each border strip.

5. Position and appliqué the leaves over the accent strip using the illustration below and the photograph as a placement guide. We suggest that you appliqué just 4 of the leaves to the top and bottom borders; wait until after sewing the borders to the quilt to add the leaves at the corners. Then you can place them over the mitered border seams. You'll see that we didn't include the reverse appliqué in the center of each leaf. We're not from Emporia!

Note: *Be sure to change the direction of the leaves in the center of the top and bottom borders.*

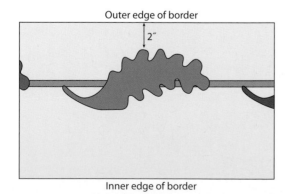

6. Sew the borders to the quilt, mitering the corners. (Refer to Mitered Border Corners, page 60, as needed.)

7. Appliqué the remaining leaves to the border.

Quilt assembly

Quilting and Finishing

1. Quilt around the outside of each appliqué image—flowers, stems, leaves—to puff up the appliqué. Typical Emporia quilting has few lines on the appliqué pieces. For more information, refer to the quilting details that follow and see Quilting Inspired by Emporia (page 61).

To quilt inside the appliqué shapes, see the suggested quilting lines included on each block pattern.

2. After quilting is complete, make and add the binding using the yellow strips.

MARKING THE NEW ROSE WREATH BLOCKS

Start by marking fancy quilting motifs in the New Rose Wreath blocks. The block pattern (pullout page P1) includes a floral design to quilt in the center background of the blocks. For additional fancy quilting patterns to stitch into the rest of the block background, see patterns for New Rose Wreath feather and fleur-de-lis (pullout page P2).

1. Trace the fleur-de-lis shapes in all 4 corners of the 4 blocks.

2. Trace the feather unit on 3 edges of each block, fitting the feather outside the appliquéd wreath and overlapping the block seamline as shown in the pattern.

Note: *Do not trace the feather on the outside edge of the blocks (next to the border) because it won't fit with the border quilting. The exception is the block that falls above the bouquet in the bottom border. It will fit there.*

New Rose Wreath quilting pattern placement

Use Quilting to Blend Backgrounds
The quilting design overlaps the block seamline for this pattern. Quilting over the seamline helps to unify the backgrounds and integrate the blocks into the overall design.

MARKING THE BORDER
To mark the border, use the patterns for border feathers and border corners (pullout page P2).

1. Trace the border feather scallop and corner scallop onto paper to make a master pattern.

2. Trace the feather scallop backward on a separate sheet of paper to make a reverse design.

3. Mark these units alternately in the side and top borders between the block seamlines and the appliquéd leaves. The feathers are a little longer than 10″ each, so you can fit 2 along each 21″ block.

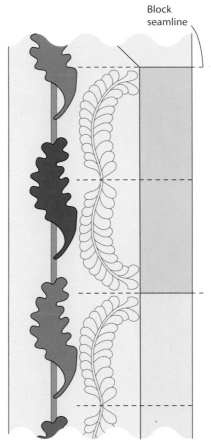

Mark feathers in border.

4. On the bottom border, trace a pair of feathers under the left and right blocks. The feathers won't fit between the center block and the top of the border bouquet. This is where the New Rose Wreath feather will fill the space.

MARKING THE FILLER QUILTING
The fancy motifs are only part of the quilting. To get the old-fashioned look, fill in behind the decorative designs with a lined background pattern. Mark the filler design in the blank spaces around each block and border appliqué after you've marked the more elaborate quilting designs. See Quilting Inspired by Emporia (page 61) for a sampling of filler designs used by quilters of the era.

Made by Barbara Brackman and Pam Mayfield, quilted by Pam Mayfield, 2010

Perennial Poppy

Finished quilt: 48″ × 48″ | **Finished block:** 18″

Barbara hand appliquéd four Oriental Poppy blocks, omitting the reverse appliqué in the leaves and flowers. Pam added the sawtooth borders and machine quilted it. We updated the color scheme of the original quilt with poppy oranges and dark aqua batik prints. These complementary colors—red-orange and blue-green—are directly across the color wheel from each other.

Fabric Requirements and Cutting Instructions

Because the appliqué process tends to shrink blocks and borders slightly, the background pieces are cut oversized. You will trim them to size after the appliqué is finished. For more information about preparing and cutting the background fabric, see Fabric Preparation (page 56). Yardage is based on 42″-wide fabric.

Before tracing and cutting appliqué shapes, see Appliqué (page 56). Refer to the patterns (pullout page P3) and to the color photo of the quilt (previous page) as a guide to color placement.

PERENNIAL POPPY

Fabric	For	Cutting
¾ yard each of 3 dark aquas and 1¼ yards of a fourth dark aqua	Block background	1 square 20″ × 20″ from each fabric
	Sawtooth border	7 squares 3⅞″ × 3⅞″ from each fabric (28 total)
	Outer border	2 strips 3½″ × 21½″ from each fabric (8 total)
	Binding	6 strips 2½″ × width of fabric from the fourth dark aqua
8 fat quarters medium oranges	Large flowers, small flowers, and center circles	See patterns (pullout page P3).
	Sawtooth border	3 squares 3⅞″ × 3⅞″ from each fabric (24 total)
4 fat eighths light oranges	Reverse appliqué and small circles	See patterns (pullout page P3).
	Sawtooth border	1 square 3⅞″ × 3⅞″ from each fabric (4 total)
4 fat quarters light and medium blue-greens	Leaves and stems	See patterns (pullout page P3).
3⅛ yards neutral	Backing	
56″ × 56″ batting		

Simplify the Appliqué

The complexity of the leaves in the *Oriental Poppy* pattern makes it one of the most difficult of the Emporia patterns. If the leaf looks intimidating, skip the reverse appliqué as Barbara did. You can make it even easier by substituting the simpler leaf pattern provided on the pullout pages. It has fewer and gentler curves and does not include reverse appliqué.

Four-Block Appliqué

1. Appliqué the Oriental Poppy block from the *Emporia Rose Sampler* (pullout page P3) onto each 20″ background square. Trim the blocks to 18½″ × 18½″, making sure that the appliqué is centered.

Perennial Poppy block—make 4.

2. Stitch the blocks together in 2 rows of 2 blocks each.

Sawtooth Border

1. Following the instructions in Piecing Sawteeth (page 56), use the orange 3⅞″ squares and dark aqua 3⅞″ squares to make 56 half-square triangles. Set 4 aside for the outer border.

Make 56.

2. Stitch a row of 12 half-square triangles, all facing the same direction, as shown. Make 4 rows.

Make 4.

3. Sew a border strip to 2 opposite sides of the quilt so that the aqua triangles are next to the blocks.

4. Add a half-square triangle to each of the remaining border strips, as shown.

Make 2.

5. Add the strips from Step 4 to the top and bottom of the quilt, keeping the aqua triangles next to the appliquéd blocks.

Achieving the Look of the Antique Quilt

To make this small quilt look more like the original, Barbara appliquéd the design onto a background block that finishes at 18″ rather than 21″ as in *Emporia Rose Sampler* (page 30). This gives a more crowded feel to the appliqué, much like the quilts made in Rose Kretsinger's time.

Outer Border

1. Sew the 3½″ × 21½″ dark aqua strips together in pairs to make 4 outer border strips. Sew a strip to 2 opposite sides of the quilt center.

2. Add a half-square triangle to each end of the remaining 2 dark aqua strips, referring to the assembly diagram (at right). Add the strips to the top and bottom of the quilt.

Quilting and Finishing

1. Quilt around the outside of each appliqué image—each rose and each stem—to puff up the appliqué. Typical Emporia quilting has few lines on the appliqué pieces. For more details, see Quilting Inspired by Emporia (page 61).

2. Make and add the binding using the dark aqua strips.

Quilt assembly

Invite Rose Kretsinger to the Dinner Table, 22½″ × 23″, made by Denniele Bohannon, quilted by Angela Walters, 2013

Made by Karla Menaugh, quilted by Lori Kukuk, 2012

Pennsylvania Garden

Finished quilt: 54″ × 54″

Karla placed the Pennsylvania Beauty block on point and worked out a border based on Rose Kretsinger's unfinished quilt top, *Pennsylvania Beauty* (page 22). Rose had noted her fabric choices as "old calico" and lavender, but Karla pushed the colors to the other side of the color wheel, using reds and red-orange with a touch of greenish yellow in the center circles. Rather than using prints, she updated the look, cutting her appliqué from solid fabrics with just a touch of pattern in the weave.

Marketed today as *shot cottons*, these almost-solids are cloths with different warp and weft colors. The weaving technique was often used with silk in the past, the resulting fabric known as *changeable silk* because of the way the color changed when the light hit the fabric at different angles—think taffeta. Another name is *shot silk* because one throw of the bobbin is "a shot" carrying a single weft thread over the warp thread.

Fabric Requirements and Cutting Instructions

Because the appliqué process tends to shrink blocks and borders slightly, the center background is cut oversized. You will trim the block to size after the appliqué is finished. For more information about preparing and cutting the background fabric, see Fabric Preparation (page 56). Yardage is based on 42″-wide fabric.

Before tracing and cutting appliqué shapes, see Appliqué (pages 56). Refer to the patterns (pullout pages P3 and P4) and to the color photo of the quilt (previous page) to guide color placement.

PENNSYLVANIA GARDEN

Fabric	For	Cutting
3¼ yards yellow	Block background	1 square 41″ × 41″
	Border background	2 squares 30″ × 30″; cut each in half diagonally to make 2 triangles, 4 total
	Binding	4 strips 2½″ × 58″
⅓ yard dark red	Flowers, buds, and berries	See *Pennsylvania Beauty* block and border patterns (pullout pages P3 and P4).
⅓ yard dark pink	Flowers, buds, and berries	
⅝ yard orange	Flowers, buds, and berries	
8″ square yellow/green	Flower centers	
1 yard dark green	Leaves and vines	
½ yard medium green	Leaves and vines	
3½ yards neutral	Backing	
62″ × 62″ batting		

Making the Quilt

1. Appliqué the Pennsylvania Beauty block from *Emporia Rose Sampler* (pullout page P3) onto the 41″ background square.

2. Making sure the appliqué is centered, trim the block to $38^{11}/_{16}″ × 38^{11}/_{16}″$ ($^{11}/_{16}″$ is halfway between ⅝″ and ¾″ on a ruler).

3. Stitch a border background triangle to each side of the center square.

4. Stitch the border appliqué motifs to each border, noting that the pattern falls across the seamline onto the center block. Trim and square up the quilt to 54½″ × 54½″.

Quilt assembly

Quilting and Finishing

1. Quilt around the outside of each appliqué image—each rose and each stem—to puff up the appliqué.

Typical Emporia quilting has few lines on the appliqué pieces. For more details, see Quilting Inspired by Emporia (page 61).

2. Make and add the binding using the yellow strips.

Made by Karla Menaugh, quilted by Lori Kukuk, 2012

Anna's Thistle

Finished quilt: 85¾″ × 100″ | **Finished block:** 10″

Double Irish Chain and Scotch Thistle (page 27) was the inspiration for this quilt. We loved Anna Good's use of an Irish Chain as an appliqué frame and her color contrasts, faded and mellowed over the years. Anna appliquéd a Scotch thistle, but Karla, raised a Kansas farmer, just can't glorify a noxious weed. We found an appealing and folksy floral in the border of a nineteenth-century quilt and appliquéd that in the blocks instead. For an alternative very like Anna's thistle appliqué design, see Thistle and Buds Pincushions (page 50).

Fabric Requirements and Cutting Instructions

Because the appliqué process tends to shrink blocks and borders slightly, the background pieces are cut oversized. You will trim them to size after the appliqué is finished. For more information about preparing and cutting the background fabric, see Fabric Preparation (page 56). Yardage is based on 42″-wide fabric.

Before tracing and cutting appliqué shapes, see Appliqué (page 56). Cut the lengthwise border strips first, about 2″ longer than indicated, and measure your quilt before cutting them to the final length.

ANNA'S THISTLE

Fabric	For	Cutting
5 yards light neutral	25-Patch blocks	8 strips 2½″ × width of fabric
	Appliqué block background	20 squares* 7″ × 7″ 7 strips 2½″ × width of fabric; subcut into 40 rectangles 2½″ × 6½″ 3 strips 6½″ × width of fabric
	Side setting triangles	5 squares* 9¾″ × 9¾″; cut each in quarters diagonally to make 4 triangles, 20 total (2 are extra) 9 strips 2½″ × width of fabric; subcut into 36 rectangles 2½″ × 8½″
	Corner setting triangles	2 squares* 8″ × 8″; cut each in half diagonally to make 2 triangles, 4 total
	Border 1*	2 strips 3″ × 85⅜″ 2 strips 3″ × 76¼″
3⅜ yards medium orange	25-Patch blocks	22 strips* 2½″ × 42″ 2 strips 2½″ × width of fabric
	Appliqué blocks	6 strips 2½″ × width of fabric
	Side setting triangles	18 squares* 2½″ × 2½″
	Border 2*	2 strips 3″ × 90⅜″ 2 strips 3″ × 81¼″
2¾ yards brown floral	25-Patch blocks	18 strips* 2½″ × 42″
	Border 3*	2 strips 3″ × 95⅜″ 2 strips 3″ × 86¼″
1 fat eighth dark orange	Appliqué buds	See *Anna's Thistle* appliqué patterns (pullout page P1).
½ yard green	Appliqué stems and sepals	
⅞ yard brown print	Binding	10 strips 2½″ × width of fabric
8 yards neutral	Backing	
94″ × 108″ batting		

* Cut the border strips lengthwise first, adding 2″ to each length. Cut the asterisked squares/strips from the remaining lengthwise piece of fabric. Then cut width-of-fabric pieces from the remaining full-width yardage.

The editors at *Priscilla Patchwork* recommended a modern and rather austere approach to appliqué in 1925 for this unquilted spread. Anna adopted the design idea but used a more traditional approach.

25-Patch Blocks

1. Sew 2 brown, 2 orange, and 1 light neutral 2½″ × width of fabric strips together to make a strip set as shown. Make 4. Crosscut the strip sets into 60 segments 2½″ × 10½″.

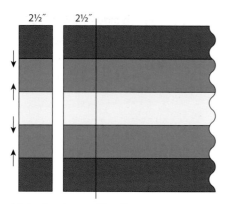

Make 4 strip sets. Cut 60 segments.

2. Sew 2 brown and 3 orange 2½″ × width of fabric strips together to make a strip set. Make 4. Crosscut the strip sets into 60 segments 2½″ × 10½″.

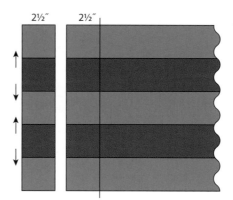

Make 4 strip sets. Cut 60 segments.

3. Sew 1 brown, 2 orange, and 2 light neutral strips together to make a strip set as shown. Make 2. Crosscut the strip sets into 30 segments 2½″ × 10½″.

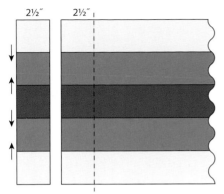

Make 2 strip sets. Cut 30 segments.

4. Stitch the segments together as shown to make the 25-Patch block. Make 30 blocks.

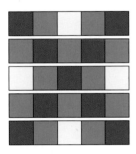

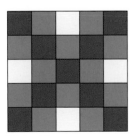

Make 30.

Appliqué Blocks

1. Appliqué a floral design to each of the light neutral 7″ squares. Use your favorite appliqué technique. For more information about our techniques, see Appliqué (page 56). Trim the blocks to 6½″ square, making sure that the design is centered.

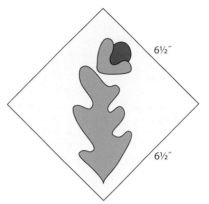

Make 20.

2. Stitch a 2½″ orange strip to each side of a 6½″ light neutral strip to make a strip set. Make 3. Crosscut the strip sets into 40 rectangles 2½″ × 10½″ with orange squares at both ends.

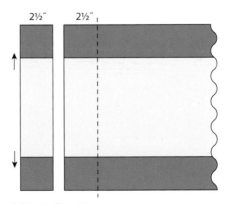

Make 3. Cut 40 segments.

3. Sew a 2½″ × 6½″ light neutral rectangle to 2 opposite sides of each floral block. Sew a pieced rectangle from Step 2 onto each of the remaining sides of the block. Repeat for all 20 blocks.

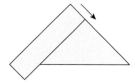

Make 20.

Setting Triangles

1. Stitch a 2½″ × 8½″ light neutral strip to a short side of a 9¾″ side setting triangle.

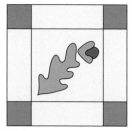

2. Stitch a 2½″ orange square to a 2½″ × 8½″ light neutral strip.

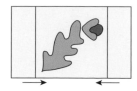

3. Sew the strip from Step 2 to the other short side of the setting triangle as shown. Trim the ends of both background strips at an angle

so that they are even with the edge of the triangle. Repeat the steps to make 18 side setting triangles.

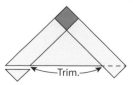

Make 18.

Quilt Assembly

1. Arrange the blocks and setting triangles in diagonal rows as shown in the quilt assembly diagram.

2. Stitch the blocks together in diagonal rows. Sew the rows together.

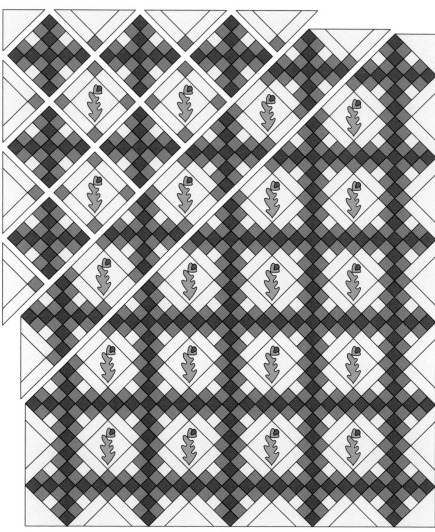

Quilt assembly

Borders

It's always a good idea to measure your quilt through the center first before cutting and adding the borders. The dimensions given are correct, but individual cutting and stitching can result in variations from the measurements below.

1. Stitch a 3″ × 85⅜″ light neutral border strip to each side of the quilt.

2. Stitch a 3″ × 76¼″ light neutral border strip to the top and the bottom of the quilt.

3. Stitch a 3″ × 90⅜″ orange border strip to each side of the quilt.

4. Stitch a 3″ × 81¼″ orange border strip to the top and the bottom of the quilt.

5. Stitch a 3″ × 95⅜″ brown floral border strip to each side of the quilt.

6. Stitch a 3″ × 86¼″ brown floral border strip to the top and the bottom of the quilt.

Quilting and Finishing

1. Quilt around the outside of each flower bud and the leaves to puff up the appliqué. Typical Emporia quilting has few lines on the appliqué pieces. For more details, see Quilting Inspired by Emporia (page 61).

2. Make and add the binding using the brown print strips.

Made by Karla Menaugh, quilted by Kelly Cline, 2013

Spice Pink Table Runner

Finished table runner: 12″ × 44″

Border detail of *Spice Pink* (page 14)

Add some updated tradition to your table with our Spice Pink runner in the spiciest pinks you can find. We've adapted the floral vine that Charlotte Whitehill used to frame her *Spice Pink* quilt (page 14) to fit this table runner. In Bonus Ideas (pages 52–55) you'll also find instructions for using the vine as an alternate border for an *Emporia Rose Sampler* or a *Spice Pink* variation.

Fabric Requirements and Cutting Instructions

Because the appliqué process tends to shrink the background slightly, the background is cut oversized. You will trim it to size after the appliqué is finished. For more information about preparing and cutting the background fabric, see Fabric Preparation (page 56). Yardage is based on 42″-wide fabric.

Before tracing and cutting appliqué shapes, be sure to read Appliqué (page 56). Refer to the color photo of the quilt (previous page) as a guide to color placement.

SPICE PINK TABLE RUNNER

Fabric	For	Cutting
1½ yards white	Background	1 rectangle 14″ × 47″
	Backing	1 rectangle 16″ × 50″
⅓ yard green	Long bias vine and large leaves	See patterns (pullout page P1).
1 fat quarter blue	Leaves and bias stems	
1 fat eighth blue-green	Tri-tipped leaves and bud stem	
6″ square each of 3 pinks, or use scraps	Flowers and buds	
5″ square yellow	Flower centers	
½ yard dark pink	Binding	4 strips 2½″ × width of fabric
18″ × 50″ batting		

Making the Table Runner

1. Appliqué 3 repeats of the Spice Pink border (pullout page P1) onto the white background fabric, flipping the direction of the vine in alternating sections.

2. Trim the background to 12½″ × 44½″.

44½″

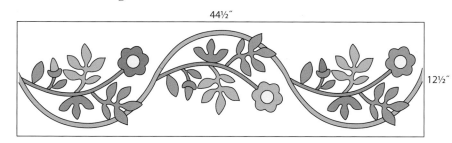

12½″

Quilting and Finishing

1. Quilt the background and stitch outside of each appliqué shape to puff up the appliqué. Typical Emporia quilting has few lines on the appliqué pieces. For more details, see Quilting Inspired by Emporia (page 61).

2. Make and add the binding using the dark pink strips.

Pillow cover made by Karla Menaugh, 2013

Social Circles Pillow

Finished pillow: 24″ × 24″

Social Circles recalls Emporia's community of quiltmakers and the network of garden societies, quilting groups, churches, and bridge clubs that drew small-town women together in the 1930s. We found this pattern of linked rings in Rose Kretsinger's *Calendula* or *Allen Rose* quilt (page 26). Rose based that quilt on one belonging to the Allen family of Topeka. She noted that Mrs. Harry Allen's mother, Anna Belle, had made it some 75 years earlier, around 1855.

Although the geometries in the pattern look quite modern, the interlocked rings are found

in several album quilts from the mid-nineteenth century. It's doubtful, however, that Florence Daugherty Allen's mother actually made the quilt. The women in that family married young, and Anna Belle Hickman Daugherty was only 62 years old in 1930 when Rose wrote that she'd made the quilt 75 years earlier. Let's hope Mrs. Daugherty never found out how old Rose thought she was!

This pattern would also make a lovely setting block in a floral sampler quilt. See Bonus Ideas (pages 52–55).

Fabric Requirements and Cutting Instructions

Because the appliqué process tends to shrink the background slightly, the background piece is cut oversized. You will trim it to size after the appliqué is finished. For more information about preparing and cutting the background fabric, see Fabric Preparation (page 56). Yardage is based on 42″-wide fabric.

Before tracing and cutting appliqué shapes, see Appliqué (page 56). Refer to the color photo of the pillow (previous page) to guide color placement.

SOCIAL CIRCLES PILLOW

Fabric	For	Cutting
2 yards dark gray solid	Background for front and back	1 square 24″ × 24″ 2 rectangles 14½″ × 23″
½ yard blue print	Border for front and back	4 strips 1¼″ × width of fabric; subcut a 23″ strip and a 15¼″ strip from each 2 strips 1¼″ × 24½″
	Rings	See *Social Circles* pattern (pullout page P3); cut 4 rings.
10″ square each of yellow, orange, and lime-green print	Rings	See *Social Circles* pattern (pullout page P3); cut 4 rings from each.
24″ pillow form		

Making the Pillow Top

1. Appliqué the rings onto the 24″ background square. You will need to cut every other ring and hide the cut ends under the adjacent ring. Trim the square to 23″ × 23″, making sure the design is centered.

2. Sew a 23″ blue strip to 2 opposite sides of the Social Circles block.

3. Sew a 24½″ blue strip to the remaining sides of the block to complete the pillow front.

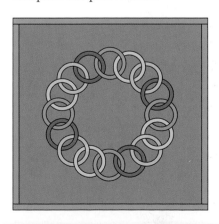

Making the Pillow Back

1. Sew a 23″ blue strip to a long side of each of the 14½″ × 23″ gray rectangles.

2. Sew a 15¼″ blue strip to each short side of the rectangles from Step 1.

3. Turn under ¼″ along the long gray side of each rectangle, and press. Fold again ¾″ and press. Topstitch ⅛″ from the inner folded edge of each to create a hem.

Pillow Assembly

1. Place the pillow front faceup on a flat surface.

2. Place a pillow back rectangle facedown on top of the pillow front, lining up the blue borders on the back with the blue borders on one side of the front. Pin.

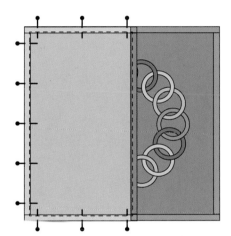

3. Place the remaining pillow back facedown on the other side of the pillow front, matching the blue borders with the pillow top. The rectangles will overlap in the center.

4. Stitch a ¼″ seam around the outside edge of the pillow.

5. Trim the corners at a diagonal and turn the pillow right side out.

6. Insert the pillow form.

Oriental Poppy

Made by Karla Menaugh, 2013

Scotch Thistle

Thistle and Buds Pincushions

Tomato Buds

Finished pincushions:

Oriental Poppy, 4½″ × 7″ | Scotch Thistle, 8″ × 8″ | Tomato Buds, 3⅜″

These sweet little pincushions are the perfect projects for a rainy afternoon. We keep several small pincushions like the Oriental Poppy and Tomato Buds attached to our design walls. Stuffed lightly with wool roving, they are lightweight and handy, keeping pins in reach for pinning projects to the wall. The Scotch Thistle is a nice size for a sewing table. It can be stuffed with wool roving or play sand.

The *Scotch Thistle* pattern is nearly identical to the one in Anna Good's *Double Irish Chain and Scotch Thistle* (page 27). We've sized it not only for the pincushion but also as a design alternative for the floral appliqué in *Anna's Thistle* (page 40).

Fabric Requirements and Cutting Instructions

These projects use felted wool, which is very easy to work with. There's no need to add seam allowances or turn under the edges, since it will not ravel. Refer to the pincushion patterns and to the photos (previous page) as a guide to color placement.

Making the Pincushions

SCOTCH THISTLE PINCUSHION

1. Appliqué the design onto the oatmeal background rectangle.

2. Center the rectangle on the green background rectangle. Stitch by machine just inside the edge of the oatmeal background.

3. Center and sew the unit to an 8½″ square of coral cotton background fabric.

4. Place the stitched unit from Step 3 right sides together with the second 8½″ square of coral cotton. Stitch ¼″ around the outside edge of the squares, leaving a small opening in the center along the bottom.

5. Trim the corners at a diagonal and turn the pincushion right side out.

6. Stuff with wool roving and sew the opening closed by hand.

Optional: If you want to stuff the pincushion with play sand, make a lining by sewing 2 additional 8½″ cotton squares together. Place the lining inside the pincushion, fill

THISTLE AND BUDS PINCUSHIONS

Fabric	For	Cutting
Scotch Thistle		
1 fat quarter coral cotton	Background 3 and backing	2 squares 8½″ × 8½″
9″ square mottled green wool	Background 2	1 square 6¾″ × 6¾″
9″ square oatmeal wool	Background 1	1 square 6″ × 6″
6″ square green wool	Stem and leaves	See *Scotch Thistle* pattern (pullout page P3).
Scraps of red and yellow wool	Thistle blossom	
Oriental Poppy		
1 fat sixteenth blue-purple wool	Background 2	1 rectangle 4½″ × 7″
Scrap of black wool	Background 1	1 rectangle 3½″ × 6″
Scraps of dark pink, orange, yellow, and green wool	Flower, stem, and leaves	See *Oriental Poppy* border pattern (pullout page P1).
Tomato Buds		
Scrap of yellow-green wool	Background 2	1 circle 4⅜″ diameter
Scrap of purple wool	Background 1	1 circle 4″ diameter
Scraps of green and orange wool	Buds and stems	See the buds on the *Tomato Flower* pattern (pullout page P2).

Wool roving or play sand (see Resources, page 62)

with sand, and sew the openings closed by hand.

ORIENTAL POPPY PINCUSHION

1. Appliqué the poppy design onto the black wool rectangle.

2. Center the rectangle right side up on the purple background rectangle. Using a straight stitch, sew the top rectangle to the background, leaving a small opening at the bottom.

Leave open.

3. Stuff a small amount of wool roving into the

pincushion through the opening, and then sew the opening closed.

TOMATO BUDS PINCUSHION

1. Appliqué the tomato buds and stems onto the purple wool 4″ circle.

2. Center the circle right side up on the yellow-green background circle. Sew the top circle to the background, leaving a small opening at the bottom.

3. Stuff a small amount of wool roving into the pincushion and sew the opening closed.

Bonus Ideas

By selecting your favorite blocks and a setting option, you can make a quilt very much like the original inspiration quilt, or you can create a unique design that reflects your personality. We were inspired to mock up some virtual quilts using the new Emporia Rose blocks in settings that come close to those of the original Emporia quilts.

Quilts with On-Point Sets

For an exciting quilt setting, turn the blocks on point and set them together in diagonal rows. Several of the Emporia-inspired quilts used this technique.

SPICE PINK VARIATION

98¼″ × 98¼″

> **Inspired by Charlotte Whitehill's *Spice Pink* (page 14)**
>
> - 17½″ finished blocks in an on-point 9 + 4 setting
> - 9 Spice Pink blocks (pullout pages P1 and P2)
> - 4 New Rose Wreath blocks (pullout page P1)
> - 12″ finished border, 5 repeats of Spice Pink border per side (pullout page P1)

In the original quilt, Charlotte made a border vine featuring a smaller version of the flower and bud in the block. For this quilt, use our version of the Spice Pink border, flipping the pattern back and forth five times on each side. Continue the vine into the corners and appliqué the flower, stem, and leaves inside the curves. The quilt center will measure 74¾″ square before the borders are added.

HEIRLOOM TOMATO FLOWER

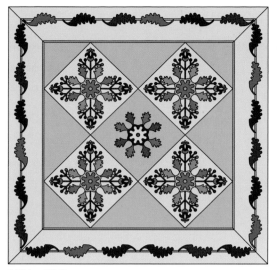

81½″ × 81½″

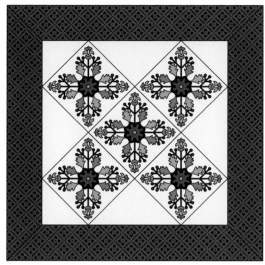

A lovely print fabric can be an alternative design choice to an appliquéd border. In this case, the quiet purple border highlights and enhances the complexity of the appliqué and colors in the Tomato Flower blocks.

To appliqué the outer border, follow the guidelines in Borders (pages 32), but cut the border background strips 10½″ wide and line up the 1½″ folded border accent strip so the raw edges of the strip are 4½″ from the outer edge of the border. The ½″-wide finished strip will be 5¾″ from the inside raw edge of the border and 4¼″ from the outside raw edge of the border. The quilt center will measure 60″ square before the borders are added.

Quilts with Straight Sets

ANTIQUE ORIENTAL POPPY

86″ × 86″

You would expect the side border swags to line up with the outer edges of the saw-tooth border, but Rose fitted them between the first and second sawteeth at each corner, perhaps to make more room for her corner swags. The tri-tipped leaves at the top of each swag are made separately so that you can adjust the space between the swags to fit your border and then cover the top of each space with the leaves.

EMPORIA ROSE WITH SPICE PINK BORDER

84″ × 84″

All the sampler blocks from *Emporia Rose Sampler* (page 30) with a border inspired by *Spice Pink* (page 14)

- 21″ finished blocks in a straight 3 × 3 setting

- 5 sampler blocks (pullout pages P1–P4)

- 4 New Rose Wreath blocks (pullout page P1)

- 10½″ finished border, 5 repeats per side of Spice Pink border (reduced) (pullout page P1)

To make a quilt with this look, copy the Spice Pink border at 85%, so that it is 12⅝″ long. Flip the pattern back and forth 5 times on each side. Continue the vine into the corners and appliqué the flower, stem, and leaves inside the curves. The quilt center will measure 63½″ square before the borders are added.

FOUR-BLOCK APPLIQUÉ SAMPLER

48″ × 48″

Choose 4 sampler blocks from *Emporia Rose Sampler* (page 30) and add a sawtooth border.

- 18″ finished blocks in a straight 2 × 2 setting

- 52 sawteeth finishing at 3″ for inner border (see Piecing Sawteeth, page 56)

- 3″ outer border with 4 sawtooth corners (total of 56 sawteeth)

Follow instructions for *Perennial Poppy* (page 34), but make 4 blocks of your choice.

Design Your Own Quilt

Use the *Emporia Rose Sampler* blocks in any combination to make your own quilt design. You can make the block backgrounds 21″ as we did in the sampler, creating ample space for quilting in each block. Or you can let the appliqué design fill the block by trimming it to as small as 17½″ finished, which leaves only ¼″ to ½″ of space around the appliqué.

1. Choose a block size, anywhere from 17½″ to 22″ finished. Cut blocks 2″ larger than finished size.

2. For an on-point setting, use the chart (below right) to cut side setting triangles and corner setting triangles.

3. Appliqué the blocks, trim, and sew together.

4. Check the finished size of the quilt center by measuring it at the top, center, and bottom both horizontally and vertically. Subtract ½″ for the finished size.

5. Choose a border pattern and measure the length of its repeat. To see how many repeats you will need for each border, divide the finished size of the quilt center by the length of the repeat.

> *Example:* 70″ quilt center ÷ 10″ repeat = 7 repeats

FITTING A BORDER

If the number of repeats doesn't divide evenly into the size of the quilt center, there are several ways to make adjustments:

- Make the quilt center a little larger by adding a coping strip—a narrow inner border in the same fabric as the block background. The coping strip will blend into the block backgrounds and be virtually unnoticeable in the finished quilt.

  > *Example:* 70″ finished quilt center with 12″ border repeat. To make the quilt center 72″ finished to accommodate 6 border repeats, add a 1″ finished (1½″ cut) inner border strip to each side of the quilt center.

- If the predominant element of your chosen border is a vine, adjust the vine spacing by a small amount in each repeat and place the other appliqué elements to fit.

  > *Example:* 72″ quilt center ÷ 10″ repeat = 7 with 2″ left over. Divide the border background fabric into 7 equal sections. Center the border repeat in each section and make the border vine just a bit longer as it crosses each dividing line.

- For other repeating border designs, enlarge or reduce the repeat to make it fit.

  > *Example:* 70″ quilt center with 6½″ repeat = 10 repeats with 5″ left over. Enlarge the design to make the repeat 7″, to fit perfectly with 10 repeats. You may have to make the border wider to fit the larger border design.

MATH FOR ON-POINT QUILT SETTINGS

Finished block*	Finished diagonal width of block (FD)**	Squares for side setting triangles***	Squares for corner setting triangles****
17½″	24.75″	26″	13¼″
18″	25.46″	26¾″	13⅝″
19″	26.87″	28⅛″	14⅜″
20″	28.28″	29⅝″	15⅛″
21″	29.7″	31″	15¾″
22″	31.11″	32⅜″	16½″

Add 2″ when cutting to oversize the blocks; after appliquéing, trim and square up the block to ½″ larger than the finished size.

** Finished size × 1.414 = FD

*** FD + 1.25″; cut the squares in quarters diagonally.

**** (FD ÷ 2) + .875″; cut the squares in half diagonally.

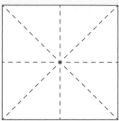

Construction Techniques

Piecing Sawteeth

Sawteeth are sometimes called half-square triangles. Refer to the project instructions for the size of the squares to cut.

1. With right sides together, pair 2 contrasting squares. Lightly draw a diagonal line from corner to corner on the wrong side of the lighter square.

Draw line.

2. Sew a scant ¼″ away on each side of the line, and then cut on the drawn line.

Sew.

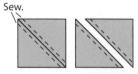

3. Press the seam toward the darker fabric and trim off the dog-ears.

Appliqué

FABRIC PREPARATION

1. Prewash all fabric in hot water and dry it in a hot dryer. This accomplishes several objectives—it shrinks the fabric as much as it will ever shrink, removes excess dye, and also removes the sizing. The latter makes the fabric softer and easier to manipulate as you create the appliqué elements.

2. Cut the background blocks and borders oversized. Appliqué often causes a block to shrink a bit, so this strategy gives you a chance to trim the block accurately after the appliqué is complete.

A good rule of thumb is to add 2″ to the finished block size to allow for shrinkage. For example, for the 21″ finished *Emporia Rose Sampler* blocks, we started with 23″ squares.

3. To aid in positioning appliqués, press placement lines in the backgrounds. Fold each block in half horizontally, vertically, and diagonally in both directions, pressing the centerline at each fold.

Fold and press placement lines into each block.

MACHINE APPLIQUÉ

We use a freezer-paper machine appliqué technique that looks a lot like hand appliqué. This is a great technique for anyone who wants to machine stitch quilts that look hand appliquéd. For information about where to buy the threads and adhesives listed in this section, see Resources (page 62).

Use thin, all-cotton thread that matches the appliqué pieces. We used DMC 50-weight Machine Embroidery Thread. Mettler 60-weight, 2-ply cotton thread and Aurifil 50-weight cotton thread are also good choices.

The machine stitch that looks the most like hand appliqué is the variable overlock. On most machines, it takes three straight stitches forward then one zigzag stitch, followed by three more straight stitches and another zigzag, and so on. To make this stitch mimic hand appliqué, override the default settings to make it much narrower and shorter.

For the best setting on your machine, compare a stitched sample with the full-size sample shown in the photo (next page). Sew in-the-ditch right along the edge of the appliqué, with the straight stitches going into the background fabric and the zigzag stitches catching the edge of the appliqué shape.

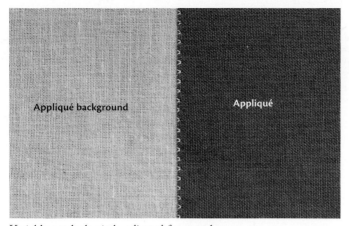

Appliqué background | Appliqué

Variable overlock stitch, adjusted for very short, very narrow stitches

To use our machine appliqué technique, follow these steps.

1. Trace the pattern pieces, without seams, onto the shiny side of freezer paper.

2. Cut them out and iron them, shiny side down, to the wrong side of the fabric. Cut out, adding a ³⁄₁₆˝ seam allowance.

3. Run a gluestick along the edge of the freezer paper and fold the fabric over the paper, leaving raw edges where any piece will be underneath another piece.

4. Position the appliqué pieces on the background and pin well. Or, better yet, baste with Roxanne Glue-Baste-It— a thin, white glue that comes in a plastic bottle with an applicator tip. Dot glue around the folded-under edges of the appliqué pieces and finger-press them into place on the background fabric. This will eliminate the bumps and ridges caused by pins.

5. Stitch by machine using the variable overlock stitch.

6. Once everything is stitched down, soak or wash the entire piece in cold water and toss it in the dryer with a dry towel. When it's dry, carefully trim the underneath fabric (background fabric) to within ¼˝ of the appliqué stitches. Remove the freezer paper and press from the wrong side. Trim the background or block to the correct size.

Using Wash-Away Paper

If you don't want to cut away the background fabric to remove freezer paper from your project, you can use Wash-Away Appliqué Sheets (by C&T Publishing) instead of the freezer paper (see Resources, page 62).

This method is a little more expensive than using freezer paper, but you won't have to cut away the background fabric to remove the paper.

1. Draw appliqué motifs or print them on the appliqué paper with an inkjet printer.

2. Fuse the paper to the wrong side of the appliqué fabric, following the manufacturer's instructions, and cut out each motif with a scant ¼˝ seam allowance.

3. Turn under the edges of the appliqué piece and glue in place.

4. Use the pieces just as you would use the appliqué motifs backed with freezer paper.

5. After the appliqué is finished, wash and dry the blocks and trim the backgrounds to the correct size.

MAKING BIAS VINES

Our favorite method is to use a bias tape maker. These come in a variety of sizes that are useful for everything from ¼″ stems to 1½″ or 2″ border vines. In this book, the projects have included ¼″, ⅜″, and ½″ bias vines.

1. Cut a bias strip twice as wide as the desired finished size. If you need to seam together strips to make a longer length than you can cut from your yardage, sew the seams diagonally to spread out the bulk of the seam allowance.

Use bias tape maker for bias vines.

Sewing a Diagonal Seam

1. Place the ends of the strips right sides together with the top strip perpendicular to the bottom strip.

2. Sew a diagonal seam from the point where the strips cross at the top left to the point where they cross at the bottom right. Check to be sure the strip opens correctly, and then trim and press the seam allowance to the side.

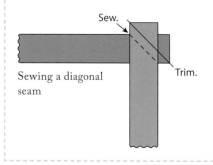

Sewing a diagonal seam

---

2. Clip an end of the strip at an angle and spray it lightly with spray starch or sizing.

3. Feed the angled end, right side of the fabric down, into the end of the bias tape maker. Pin the top of the strip to an ironing board.

4. Pull the bias tape maker along the bias strip, keeping the strip centered as it enters the tape maker.

5. Follow just behind the tape maker with a hot, dry iron. Pull the tape maker carefully so you won't stretch the bias strip. The tape maker will fold under both edges of the strip, and the hot iron will press them into place.

6. Allow the bias strip to cool for a few minutes before placing it on a block or border.

7. If you are not going to use the tape immediately, store it by winding it around a cardboard square or tube.

PLACING APPLIQUÉ ELEMENTS ON THE BACKGROUND FABRIC

To help with pattern placement, make a placement template.

1. Photocopy the pattern onto a heavy piece of paper or trace it onto the dull side of a piece of freezer paper, including the horizontal and vertical guidelines.

2. Cut some or all of the appliqué elements away from the pattern. This creates a "negative-space" template for the pattern placement. See Making Negative-Space Templates (next page).

3. Press horizontal, vertical, and diagonal guidelines into the background square.

4. Lay the background fabric on a flat surface. Line up the horizontal, vertical, and diagonal guidelines of the template with the corresponding lines on the background fabric.

5. Place appliqué elements up against the lines of the pattern, starting with elements that need to be tucked under other pieces.

Making Negative-Space Templates

Determining exactly which appliqué elements to cut away depends on which part of the block or border you need to place.

For simple blocks, such as the ones in *Anna's Thistle* (page 40), you can make a placement template for the entire block. Trace the design elements and cut them out, leaving the placement lines around them. Place the template on the center of the block, lining up all the placement guidelines, and place your appliqués in the negative space.

Place appliqués in cut-out space.

For blocks that have a repeated design in each quarter, such as *Emporia Rose Sampler* (page 30), make a template for a quarter of the block, making sure to include the horizontal, vertical, and diagonal placement lines of the template.

Match the template guidelines with the corresponding lines on the background fabric and place the design elements.

Move the placement template to an adjoining quarter of the background fabric and place the design elements for that quarter. Continue

around the block until you have placed all the appliqué pieces.

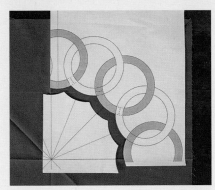
Copy block pattern and cut apart along line where design elements should be placed.

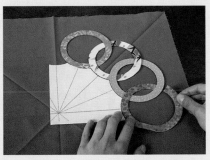
Place appliqué shapes for a quarter of the block. Move template to next quarter and repeat.

For complicated borders, such as those in *Pennsylvania Garden* (page 38), use two or more separate placement templates. In these situations, it's helpful to make the placement template on freezer paper and iron it directly onto the quilt background. The freezer paper is easy to remove and reposition.

The first template should include the seamline between the quilt center and the border and often can include all the elements up to a vine that winds its way along the center of the border. After

matching the lines on the template and on the fabric background, place all the design pieces. Remove the template and reposition it onto the next border section.

Placement guide for appliqué pieces along seamline

To complete the border's outer elements, make as many small placement templates as you need. For these, you may use other appliqué elements as placement guides. For *Pennsylvania Garden*, we used a small template to help place the berries consistently along the narrow vines.

Placement guide for berries along vine

Mitered Border Corners

1. Measure the length of the quilt top through the center and add 2 times the cut width of the border, plus 5″. Repeat for the width of the quilt top. These are the lengths you need to cut or piece the 4 borders.

2. Place pins at the centers of both side borders and the sides of the quilt top. From the center pin, measure in both directions and mark half of the measured length of the quilt top on both side borders.

3. Pin the side borders to the quilt top, matching centers and the marked length of the side border with the edges of the quilt top. Stitch the strips to the sides of the quilt top by starting and stopping ¼″ from the beginning and end of the quilt top and backstitching at each end. The excess length of the side borders will extend beyond each edge. Press the seams toward the borders.

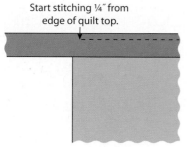

Start stitching ¼″ from edge of quilt top.

Stop stitching ¼″ from edge.

4. Repeat Steps 2 and 3 for the top and bottom borders.

5. To create the miter, lay the corner on the ironing board with the quilt right side up. Lay a border strip on top of the adjacent border.

Layer border strips.

6. Fold the top border strip under itself so that it meets the edge of the adjacent border and forms a 45° angle. Pin the fold in place.

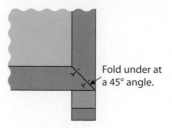

Fold under at a 45° angle.

7. Position a 90° angle triangle or ruler over the corner to check that the corner is flat and square. When everything is in place, press the fold firmly.

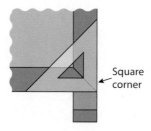

Square corner

8. Open up the quilt corner to align the creases right sides together, folding the quilt top diagonally from the corner. Pin and stitch along the fold line, starting at the inner corner, ¼″ from the seam intersection, backstitching at the beginning and end. Check that the miter is flat and smooth, and then trim the seam allowance ¼″ beyond the stitching line. Press seams open.

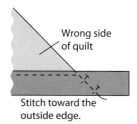

Wrong side of quilt

Stitch toward the outside edge.

Quilting Inspired by Emporia

Typical Emporia quilting has few lines quilted directly on the appliqué pieces. We always suggest that you quilt around the outside of each appliqué shape—each flower, stem, leaf, and so on—to highlight the appliqué and give it dimension.

In addition to feathers and other fancy designs, you should fill in behind the decorative designs with a lined background pattern to get the old-fashioned, antique look. Mark the filler design in the blank spaces around each block and border appliqué after you've marked the more complex heirloom quilting designs.

Emporia quilters often used what Rose Kretsinger called "square diamonds," or a diagonal grid. They also used a "plaid," a grid of double lines. Quilting simple parallel diagonal lines is less work but also traditional. If you use diagonal lines, add interest by changing direction in every other block.

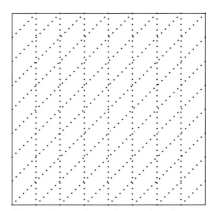

Square diamonds, or diagonal grid

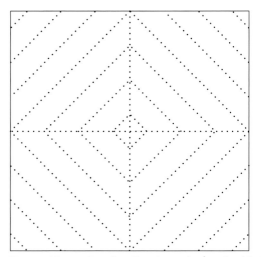

Diagonal lines, changing direction in every other block

For an authentic Emporia look, mark the lines ½″ apart. In some Emporia quilts, the lines are 5⁄16″ apart. But you can mark a grid with lines 1″ apart, and it will still look good.

When marking the grid, stop it at the point where it intersects with feathers, fleurs-de-lis, or outline quilting around the appliqué. Do not quilt over the appliqué. That's a very nineteenth-century look, but not one favored by the Emporia quilters.

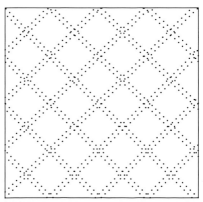

Rose Kretsinger's "plaid," a grid of double lines

Read More about Emporia Quilts

Brackman, Barbara, "Emporia 1925–1950: Reflections on a Community." In *Kansas Quilts & Quilters*, by Barbara Brackman, Jennie Chinn, Gayle R. Davis, et al. Lawrence: University Press of Kansas, 1993. The Kansas Quilt Project's findings about an unusual place and time.

Brackman, Barbara, "Rose Kretsinger." In *The Quilters Hall of Fame*, edited by Merikay Waldvogel, Rosalind Webster Perry, and Marian Ann Montgomery. Minneapolis: Voyageur Press, 2011.

Brackman, Barbara, and Ilyse Moore, *The Garden Quilt: Interpreting a Masterpiece.* Kansas City: Star Books, 2012. An updated pattern for the classic Emporia medallion.

Gregory, Jonathan, "The Joy of Beauty: The Creative Life and Quilts of Rose Kretsinger." In *Uncoverings 2007: Volume 28 of the Research Papers of the American Quilt Study Group*, edited by Joanna E. Evans. Lincoln, Neb.: American Quilt Study Group, 2007. The definitive biography.

Hall, Carrie A., and Rose G. Kretsinger, *The Romance of the Patchwork Quilt in America.* Caldwell, Idaho: Caxton Printers, 1935. Read Rose's chapter on quilting for her ideas and designs.

Resources

FOR PAPERS AND PLASTICS
by C&T Publishing: www.ctpub.com:

- Quilter's Freezer Paper Sheets
- Visi-Grid Quilter's Template Sheets
- Wash-Away Appliqué Sheets or Roll

FOR WOOL ROVING
by Clover: www.clover-usa.com

FOR MACHINE APPLIQUÉ THREADS

- DMC 50-weight Machine Embroidery Thread

  Soft Expressions: www.softexpressions.com > Thread, Yarn & Fiber > DMC Thrds: Machine & Freehand Embroidery

- Aurifil 50-weight cotton thread

  Follow That Thread: www.followthatthread.com > Products > Shop for Thread > Shop by Weight, Spool Size > 50/2

- Mettler 60-weight cotton thread

  Rushbrooke Strand: www.roserushbrooke.com > Go Shopping > Thread > Mettler > Fine Embroidery 60 Weight 219 Yds

FOR PILLOW FORMS AND GLUESTICKS
Sewing and craft stores

FOR PLAY SAND
Discount and home and garden stores

FOR ROXANNE GLUE-BASTE-IT
Stores and websites that sell quilting notions, including Connecting Threads: www.connectingthreads.com

About the Authors

Photo by Deb Rowden

Barbara Brackman and Karla Menaugh

Barbara Brackman is a quilt historian and author from Lawrence, Kansas. Well known as an authority on quilts of the Underground Railroad, Barbara has written numerous books on quilting during the Civil War, including *Facts and Fabrications: Unraveling the History of Quilts and Slavery* and her most recent C&T book, *Barbara Brackman's Civil War Sampler*. She has several blogs on quilt history, with her Civil War quilts blog getting more than a million hits since she started it two years ago. She was inducted into the Quilters Hall of Fame of Marion, Indiana, in 2001, and her C&T book *Making History* was awarded a Kansas Library Association medal in 2010. Additionally, Barbara designs reproduction fabrics for Moda and has served as a consultant on many major quilt research projects.

Karla Menaugh is a journalist and editor with experience in both newspapers and public relations. With Barbara, she managed the Sunflower Pattern Cooperative, a successful quilt pattern company, from 2000 to 2009. Barbara did the designing and drafting, and Karla collaborated on subject and design ideas, sewed many of the models, wrote the copy, and managed the business. Karla is skilled at machine quilting techniques, particularly machine appliqué, and teaches in guilds and shops. She lives near Louisville, Kentucky. She also is a freelance developmental editor for C&T Publishing.

ALSO BY BARBARA BRACKMAN:

Available as Print-On-Demand only

Available as eBook only

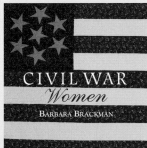

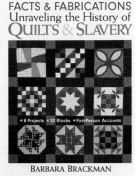

Available as Print-On-Demand and eBook only

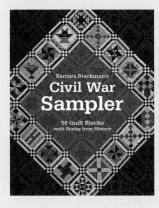

Making History

Available as eBook only

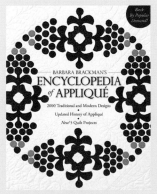

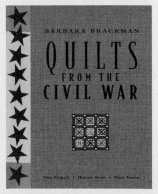

Available as eBook only

Available as Print-On-Demand and eBook only

Great Titles *from* C&T PUBLISHING